W9-BZD-356

**SCHOLASTIC**

# OVERHEAD TEACHING KIT
# Study Skills

### by Michele Goodstein

New York • Toronto • London • Auckland • Sydney
Mexico City • New Delhi • Hong Kong • Buenos Aires

Teaching
Resources

## To Erica and Jonathan

### Thanks to:

Teachers Amy Garfinkel, Michael Greenfield, Stacey Fischer, and Elaine Weinstein of Waverly Park School in the Lynbrook, N.Y. school district, who welcomed me into their classrooms and worked with me to foster better study skill strategies for their students.

Principal Barbara Hayes, for allowing me to run with a concept and supporting my efforts to introduce study skills into the curriculum.

Principal Lucille McAssey of Waverly Park School, whose persistent encouragement and gentle nudges inspired me and made this book possible.

The students of Waverly Park School, who participated in my workshops and taught me how to make them even better.

Scholastic Inc. grants teachers permission to photocopy the designated reproducible pages from this book for classroom use. No other part of this publication may be reproduced in whole or part, or stored in a retrieval system, or transmitted in any form or by any means, electronic, mechanical, photocopying, recording, or otherwise, without written permission of the publisher. For information regarding permission, write to Scholastic Inc., 557 Broadway, New York, NY 10012.

Cover Design by Jason Robinson

Design by Ellen Matlach for Boultinghouse & Boultinghouse, Inc.

Interior Illustrations by Michael Moran

Book ISBN: 0-439-70059-0
Product ISBN 0-439-44512-4

Copyright © 2004 by Scholastic Inc. All rights reserved.

Printed in the U.S.A.

3  4  5  6  7  8  9  10    40  11  10  09  08  07  06  05

# CONTENTS

# Introduction

In my six years of teaching high school, it became apparent that my students' repertoire of learning strategies was extremely limited. I frequently wondered why students didn't have any tricks up their sleeves; why they couldn't find alternative ways of getting answers when they were stumped; and why they hadn't yet learned strategies that would help them to be effective learners. While I knew that I couldn't possibly teach students everything they needed to know, I knew I had to teach them *how* to learn.

Inspired by this experience, I promised myself that if I ever began teaching at the elementary and middle school levels, I would not let a class graduate without each of its students knowing the strategies and possessing the skills of successful lifelong learners. Therefore, when I did begin teaching at those levels, I developed new ways of teaching students to be actively involved in their learning and to make connections and associations on their own. I spent seven years researching, creating, and then field-testing this program. Along the way, I worked with wonderful teachers who demonstrated better, more efficient ways of helping students access, organize, and master information.

This collection of lessons is a vehicle for helping students develop invaluable study habits and skills to carry into adulthood. Through this approach, students learn that making positive choices will help them become more successful and independent learners. The strategies in this program are based on current educational theories of brain-compatible learning, ensuring that students will be fully and actively engaged, while making their own associations and using skills applicable across the curriculum. As students see real results, they continue to employ strategies that make learning easier. While not every strategy works for all, students eventually learn to choose strategies that benefit them and fit their own learning style. The ultimate goal is to have students internalize as many skills and strategies as they can.

The best measures of the success of this program are the students who return to share their stories with me. They comment on how easy it is to plan long-term projects and stay organized and how much easier it is to learn new vocabulary— proof that the program is effective. Another measure of success is the feedback from parents who describe their child's increasingly independent study skills and report less anxiety and fewer arguments over homework assignments. The best result, however, is that my teaching has become more about *how* and less about *what* students are learning.

Once students are empowered by effective learning strategies, they learn how to approach their work and are better able to independently transfer and interact with the information they need to know. You will find that these strategies can be incorporated into all areas of the curriculum. Because I believe that all children can learn, as long as we give them the tools they need, using these activities will give you the means to accomplish this. Enjoy!

### Tips for How to Use This Book

Throughout this book, you will see transparency icons **1** marked next to certain activities. These transparencies can be found in the envelope glued inside the front cover. Using these transparencies during an introduction to a particular study skill will help students gain a deeper understanding of the skill, by seeing it in practice. This will also help them when they later work on the corresponding reproducible activities. Since each of the activities in this book is conducive to whole-class participation, you may also want to copy some of the other reproducible sheets onto clear transparencies to model some of the questions and to help students work through the answers.

# CHAPTER 1

# Setting Goals and Priorities—
## Learning to Do First Things First

For students, success in your class and in the years to come requires them to "own" their work. They must learn to prioritize tasks and activities. For example, if there is a math test on Wednesday, and a spelling quiz on Friday, they must decide which one to study for first, as well as when and how to study. They must even decide *whether* they will study. In other words, students must have a sense that they are in control, that their decisions and actions have a crucial impact on their lives. They must learn the process of establishing a goal, and creating and following through on a plan to accomplish that goal. Reaching goals demands a set of skills and habits you can help students learn. This chapter is filled with activities and exercises designed to help students begin to develop and hone these skills.

**ACTIVITY 1**    DEFINING PRIORITIES

# What to Bring on a Lifeboat

Learning how to prioritize what's important is a life skill we use every day. In some situations, such as the one presented here, it is a life-saving skill! Share this activity with students to teach how to prioritize, establish criteria, make categories, and use the process of elimination to choose the best possible solutions.

## ▷ How to Begin

Ask students to imagine that their ship is sinking and they are about to escape onto a small lifeboat. How would they feel? (Hot, scared, nervous, brave, etc.) What would they need? (Lifejackets, water, food, etc.) Write their suggestions on the board or overhead.

## ▷ Using the Reproducible

Give students a copy of the *What to Bring on a Lifeboat* Reproducible (page 13). Read through the directions and the list together. Talk to them about the importance of choosing carefully. The items they choose to bring or leave behind could be crucial to their survival.

Ask students to work in groups of three to complete the assignment. Each group will need a lifeboat captain who will share the group's answers with the class and explain their reasoning.

## ▷ Sharing Ideas

After twenty minutes of group time, ask the lifeboat captains to share their group's answers. You may first want to discuss what the groups chose NOT to bring on the lifeboat. Record their answers on the board. Were there similarities between the groups' lists? Were there items the class agreed were definitely not needed? What reasons did each lifeboat captain give? Were their reasons similar or different? Then have the captains share their group's top five things to bring on a lifeboat!

## ▷▷ Extending the Activity

▶ Have students brainstorm five more items they would bring on the lifeboat. Ask them to give the purpose for each item. Would the item help them survive or get rescued?

▶ Have students brainstorm alternative uses for items on their list. For example, they could use a math textbook to learn to navigate, burn pages for fuel, or make hats from its pages to shield themselves from the sun.

▶ Ask students to write journal entries for their days on the lifeboat. Their entries should explain how they used each item they brought along.

**ACTIVITY 2**    SETTING DAILY PRIORITIES

# How to Spend a Wednesday Evening

For many young people, each day is filled with activity. From soccer practice and spelling homework to family meals and chores, there is more than enough to do. Learning how to prioritize everyday activities is a challenge even for many adults. By helping students learn to prioritize their homework and other tasks, you will be giving them a head start on success.

## ▶ How to Begin

Talk with students about their many after-school activities and responsibilities. Keep track of up to 10 responses on Transparency 1. Altogether, how many sports do students play? How many have music practice? How many have chores? Then ask them what their favorite evening activities are. Do they like playing games with their siblings, watching television, talking on the phone, or making plans for the weekend? Is there time for everything? Ask them: "How do you decide what to do with your time?" List some of their strategies on the overhead (for example, do homework first, do what my mom asks, watch one hour of television).

Ask students to imagine that these activities and responsibilities belong to one student. As a group, discuss the priority of each item. You can also consider any strategies students have suggested. Then, together create a sample "to do" list.

## ▶ Using the Reproducible

Give each student a copy of the *How to Spend a Wednesday Evening* Reproducible (page 14). Ask them to look over the activities and list them in order of importance, according to their own priorities. Remind them that they have the right to decide their own priorities, and that priorities are neither right nor wrong but lead to different outcomes, and that some may lead to better consequences than others.

## ▶ Sharing Ideas

When students have completed the activity, ask them to share their answers in groups of two or three. Are their answers similar or different? Have them work together to brainstorm possible consequences for each item on the list, using "If . . . then" sentences. For example, "If I study for the history test tonight, then I will have time to look over any parts I don't understand."

**ACTIVITY 3**    DEFINING SHORT- AND LONG-TERM GOALS

# Looking Ahead—Near and Far

Some goals have immediate results that are easy to see. For example, if my goal is to cook a delicious dinner tonight, I will be able to see and taste the result very soon! However, long-term goals are harder to reach, and their results are harder to quantify. If my goal is to become a great chef, I will need to cook many meals, and learn many new techniques and skills to reach this goal. Understanding the difference between short- and long-term goals is an important cognitive step for students. When they can make this distinction, they can begin to plan and to work towards their future.

## ▷ How to Begin

Share with students one short-term goal and one long-term goal that you have for the class. For example, you might say "A short-term goal is a goal we can achieve in the near future. One of my short-term goals for our class is to make time today to work on our art project. How do you think we can do that?" Show them a pocket chart with the schedule of the day and work together to solve the problem by moving or shortening an activity. Congratulate the class for achieving the goal.

Next, share a long-term goal you have for the class, such as learning how to write science reports, or reading six books by the end of the semester. Explain that a long-term goal takes more time to achieve and must be broken into more steps. Ask them to brainstorm the steps necessary to achieve the goal (for example, making a list of books to read, choosing six, reading one each month, staying on schedule).

## ▷ Using the Reproducible

Now that you've talked about different kinds of goals, share the *Looking Ahead* Reproducible (page 15). Ask them to read the list of goals and to work independently, marking each goal with an S, M, or L for short-, medium-, or long-term.

## ▷ Sharing Ideas

After students finish the activity, review it together. Did most or all students give the same answers to each question? Why or why not? What criteria did they use to decide upon their answers? Some of the items listed are things to do now; others are goals for the future. Help students articulate that a goal can be defined by the length of time or the number of steps it takes to achieve.

## ▷▷ Extending the Activity

▶ Have groups of students choose an item on the list and make a list of the steps that would be required to achieve it.

▶ Challenge the class to think of other ways to categorize the list of goals. Thus far, they've organized goals and priorities by importance and by term. What other ways can they discover?

**ACTIVITY 4**    SETTING GROUP GOALS

# Our Class Goals Organizer

A group of people—a club, a business, a family, or a class—has priorities and goals just as individuals do. As students learn about goal-setting, take this opportunity to talk about the daily priorities of the classroom and to help students set reachable goals for the class.

## ▶ How to Begin

Talk to students about the difference between priorities and goals—priorities are "must do's" while goals are "plan to do's." Ask them to help you make a list of priorities for the classroom, such as safety, learning, and cooperation. Work together to establish a list you can agree on. Tell students that you are all going to work together to set goals for the class, based on these priorities.

## ▶ Using the Reproducible

Give each student a copy of the *Our Class Goals Organizer* Reproducible (page 16). Ask them to work in groups of three to brainstorm five short-term goals (goals the class can meet today) that correspond with a priority. Next, each group can brainstorm goals for the month (medium-term) and the year (long-term).

## ▶ Sharing Ideas

Spend some time reviewing the ideas each group brainstormed for short-, medium-, and long-term goals. Each group member should serve as spokesperson for part of the discussion. Depending on the amount of time you have to devote to this exercise, you can set just a few goals in each category for the class or establish a set of goals to guide your class to the end of year.

## ▶▶ Extending the Activity

▶ Setting clear goals for the classroom will help students learn to set their own individual learning goals. Make a wall chart listing the medium- and long-term goals of your class. Decorate it with a soccer or hockey theme.

▶ As students reach the medium- and long-term goals you have established, recognize the achievement with a monthly class party or fun ceremony.

**ACTIVITY 5**    SETTING INDIVIDUAL GOALS

# Planning and Mapping Personal Goals

Young students often have a hard time thinking of the future. Each day brings so many new experiences that it is difficult for them to see the long-term results of daily activities. Encouraging them to spend time on a regular basis thinking or writing about their goals helps children establish habits of goal-setting and self-reflection that will be important to them throughout their lives.

## ▶ How to Begin

Explain to students that goals are personal and special. Tell them: "This is a good opportunity for you to do some thinking about your life and what you want to accomplish. You do not need to share your answers with the class." Encourage students to take this activity seriously and approach it thoughtfully.

## ▶ Using the Reproducibles

Distribute a copy of the *Mapping My Life* Reproducible (page 17) to each student. Review the sheet, explaining that there are probably many different areas in their lives where they can succeed. This activity will give them a chance to set goals in some of these areas. You may want to share a few of your own personal goals. Encourage children to use colored pencils or to draw their goals to personalize their maps.

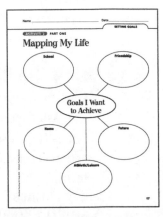

Next, give each student a copy of the *My Goals Organizer* Reproducible (page 18). Ask them to use their maps to generate personal goals and then categorize them as short-, medium-, and long-term. Be sure to have them include at least two academic goals in the short- and medium-term categories. Encourage them to think carefully about their choices.

## ▶▶ Extending the Activity

Use these sheets as a springboard for daily or weekly writing assignments. Later in the school year, distribute another copy of the *My Goals Organizer* reproducible to each student. Then give them back their earlier answers. Ask them to compare the two and write a journal entry about how their goals have changed or remained the same.

Short-term goals:
Do well on the state
social studies test.
Do more things with
my brother.
    —Jana, fifth-grader

Medium-term goals:
Get a scholarship
to college.
Make a lot of friends.
—Jackie, fifth-grader

Long-term goals:
Get a good job.
Visit every country
in Europe.
   —Felicia, fifth-grader

Name _____  Date _____

**ACTIVITY 1**

# Setting Priorities—
## What to Bring on a Lifeboat

Making careful decisions based on sound reasons is an important skill you will use every day. In some situations, this skill could even save your life.

Close your eyes and imagine that you are on a large sailboat in the ocean. Suddenly, you hit a floating log that rips a hole in the bow of the boat. You estimate that you have about fifteen minutes before the boat sinks. There is a small, inflatable lifeboat on board. You must quickly load it with the supplies that you need in order to survive. You realize that it may be days or even weeks before you are rescued.

Here is a list of items on the sailboat:

| | | | |
|---|---|---|---|
| flashlight | canned food | matches | portable radio |
| first-aid kit | fishing gear | portable grill | flares |
| dry clothes | tent | laptop computer | lifejacket |
| school books | pocket knife | suntan lotion | paddle |
| bottled water | plastic garbage bags | travelers' checks | hair dryer (battery operated) |
| batteries | | tissues | |

▶ Now list the five most essential items in order of their importance to your survival at sea. In the space next to each item, explain why you want to bring it.

**Most important items:**          **Why I chose this item:**

**1.** _____     **1.** _____

**2.** _____     **2.** _____

**3.** _____     **3.** _____

**4.** _____     **4.** _____

**5.** _____     **5.** _____

ACTIVITY 2

# How to Spend a Wednesday Evening

Each day you are faced with a wide range of things you need or want to do for school, for your family and friends, or for yourself. Below is a list of things you could possibly do on a Wednesday evening. Arrange them in the order of your priorities. Put the most important task first.

- ✔ Organize my backpack for school tomorrow
- ✔ Watch my favorite TV program
- ✔ Choose clothes to wear to school tomorrow
- ✔ Have dinner with my family
- ✔ Talk to a friend who has called to ask about the math homework
- ✔ Study for the history test being given on Friday
- ✔ Begin science report due next Monday
- ✔ Chat online with my friends
- ✔ Complete math homework problems that are due tomorrow
- ✔ Read a book of my choosing for pleasure

## "To Do" List

1. _____
2. _____
3. _____
4. _____
5. _____
6. _____
7. _____
8. _____
9. _____
10. _____

Overhead Teaching Kit: Study Skills   Scholastic Teaching Resources

**ACTIVITY 3**

# Looking Ahead

Like most people, you probably have many goals you'd like to accomplish and dreams you'd like to fulfill. Some goals can be accomplished today; others will take years.

Try categorizing the following goals as either short-, medium-, or long-term goals. Mark each goal with an **S**, **M**, or **L**.

_____  Become a professional athlete

_____  Learn to play the guitar

_____  Read a book for a book report

_____  Go on a trip around the world

_____  Hang out with my friends on Friday night

_____  Get a good grade on the next math test

_____  Go to college

_____  Buy a house

_____  Learn a new language

_____  Go to sports practice

_____  Have a family of my own

_____  Get a summer job

_____  Watch less TV so I can spend more time on homework

_____  Save enough money to buy a car

_____  Go deep-sea diving

Name_____  Date_____

**ACTIVITY 4**

# Our Class Goals Organizer

## Short-Term Goals

This week our class will:

1. _____
2. _____
3. _____
4. _____
5. _____

## Medium-Term Goals

This month our class will:

1. _____
2. _____
3. _____
4. _____
5. _____

## Long-Term Goals

Before the end of the year, our class will:

1. _____
2. _____
3. _____
4. _____
5. _____

Overhead Teaching Kit: Study Skills  Scholastic Teaching Resources

# Mapping My Life

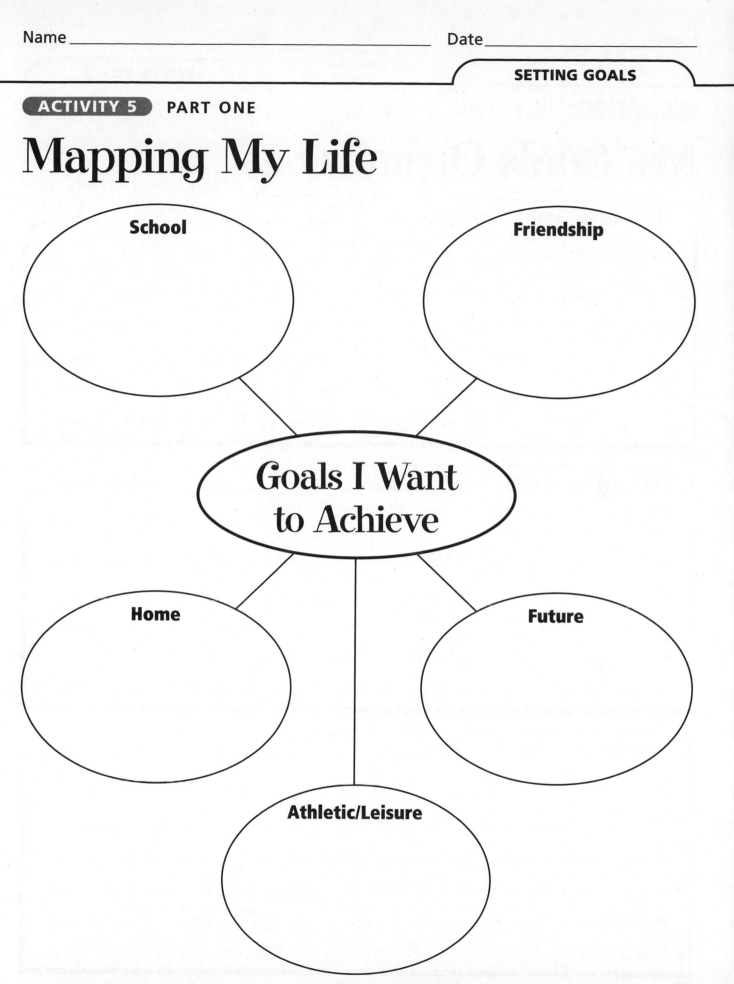

School

Friendship

## Goals I Want to Achieve

Home

Future

Athletic/Leisure

Name _____ Date _____

**ACTIVITY 5**   **PART TWO**

# My Goals Organizer

**Three of my short-term goals are:**

1. _____
_____

2. _____
_____

3. _____
_____

**Three of my medium-term goals are:**

1. _____
_____

2. _____
_____

3. _____
_____

**Three of my long-term goals are:**

1. _____
_____

2. _____
_____

3. _____
_____

Overhead Teaching Kit: Study Skills  Scholastic Teaching Resources

# CHAPTER 2

# Getting Organized—
## Creating the Right Study Environment

In a busy household, finding a quiet place at home to read and do homework can be a real challenge. Far too many students do their work in front of the television, on the living room floor, or at the computer (while listening to music and chatting online!). When students have a well-lit and organized workspace, they are far more likely to develop the daily work habits that can help them succeed in school.

This chapter is filled with activities and exercises designed to help students and their parents learn how to create a positive study environment.

**ACTIVITY 6**  RECOGNIZING INTERNAL AND EXTERNAL DISTRACTIONS

# Help! I Can't Concentrate

Everyone has trouble concentrating sometimes. When you don't feel well, or a problem is worrying you, it can be hard to give the task at hand your complete focus. But learning to concentrate—to avoid the temptation of distraction—is an important skill that we all need throughout our lives. Many students have difficulty focusing on their homework because they do not have a positive study environment where there are few distractions.

## ▶ How to Begin

Talk briefly with students about the importance of a positive study environment. Then try this simple experiment: ask them to take out their notebooks and write for five minutes about the place where they study at home. As they write, walk around the room causing distractions—hum, open a window, put on music, converse with individual students. Eventually they will catch on and laugh. Ask them to list all the things you did. These are *external* distractions. They come from outside the self.   Ask students what external distractions they experience when they do their homework. Answers may include siblings, television, traffic noise, etc.

    Then talk with students about *internal* distractions. Ask them to list distractions that come from inside themselves, such as hunger, boredom, and wishes.

## ▶ Using the Reproducible

Give each student a copy of the *Obstacles to Concentration* Reproducible (page 24). Ask them to work in groups of three to brainstorm things that keep them from concentrating. For each distraction, the group should decide if it is internal or external. Ask each group to share their list with the class. Next, each group can brainstorm solutions for each distraction.

**Encouraging students to reflect on their own learning process,** to define obstacles, and look for solutions helps them take personal responsibility. Help them see the connection between a positive study environment and success by asking questions that encourage reflection:

▶ "When you were working on your reports last night, did anyone encounter any distractions? What did you do to solve them?"

▶ "Groups, check your concentration. Are you staying on task?"

**ACTIVITY 7** DEVELOPING GOOD STUDY HABITS

# A Quiet, Well-Lit Place

A well-lit, well-stocked desk in a quiet place can make all the difference in helping a child develop good study habits. Encourage students to think about how and when they do their homework and to make a plan for creating or maintaining a homework station.

## ▶ How to Begin

Tell students, "Now that we've looked at concentration obstacles, we're each going to make a plan for a positive workspace." Share with them your own strategies. For example, you might point out that you placed your desk in a quiet(er!) corner of the classroom or tell them about the desk at home where you do your planning and grading.

## ▶ Using the Reproducible

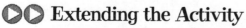

Give each student a copy of the *My Study Environment Quiz* Reproducible (page 25). Let them know that their responses to the statements won't be considered right or wrong. Encourage students to respond honestly. Then the results will help students assess their own study habits. Let them know that everyone—adults and kids—can always improve their concentration and ability to work effectively. After giving students a few minutes to complete the quiz, review their responses. Students who write *T* next to seven or more statements typically have strong study skills. A discussion about the answers may follow.

Continue by asking students to count up the number of statements they labeled as true. Ask them to record the number. Then give this quick rubric to students:

**7–8:** You have strong study skills.

**5–6:** You're on the right track!

**4 or less:** Time for a study skills overhaul!

## ▶ Sharing Ideas

Ask students if anyone would like to share his or her answer to the final question: What are your biggest obstacles to a positive work environment? Record the obstacles on the board and invite the class to brainstorm ideas to improve each situation.

## ▶▶ Extending the Activity

▶ Invite students to design the ideal homework station. What would it look like? What features would it include?

▶ If some students are in an extended-day or after-school program, talk with them and share ideas about the best ways to use the time effectively.

**ACTIVITY 8**   MAKING A STUDY PLAN

# How I Study Best

Discovering the best approach to studying is a personal process. What works very well for one student in one family environment may not work for another. With this activity, you will help students create individual study plans that can work for them.

## ▷ How to Begin

Ask students to close their eyes and visualize themselves studying. After a few moments, explain that there are many different ways to study effectively and that students can develop an individual study plan that works for them. Next, ask students to brainstorm places to study, times of day to study, and people who might be good study companions. You can keep track of their answers on the board or overhead. Encourage a brief discussion before moving on to the reproducible activity.

## ▷ Using the Reproducible

Share the *How I Study Best* Reproducible (page 26) with students. Ask them to work in pairs with one student as interviewer (recording the answers) and the other as interviewee. While you may allow students to check off more than one answer, where applicable, encourage them to think about and choose the answer that works *best* for them. Then ask each student to review his or her answers and write three things he or she plans to do to improve his or her approach to studying.

## ▷▷ Extending the Activity

▶ Have students make a bulletin board for the hallway with tips on creating a good study environment.

▶ Have the class work together to write a newsletter or study guide to share with parents and other classes.

▶ Each morning, as part of your class goal to improve study habits, ask a couple of students to share their thoughts on their study time from the previous night.

▶ Encourage students to keep a homework journal in which they record the ways in which they are staying on track, their feelings, obstacles, and so on.

**ACTIVITY 9** ORGANIZATION TIPS AND TRICKS

# Solve These Problems

Maintaining good study habits is not a simple task. It requires that students learn how to plan in advance, anticipate obstacles to studying, and make responsible decisions. Sometimes problems arise even with the best intentions. Encourage students to think about how to approach and solve the organization missteps that can occur.

## ▶ How to Begin

Talk to students about a time you faced an obstacle to getting your work done as a teacher and overcame that obstacle. For example, perhaps you left a book at home that you were planning to read to your class that day. Maybe you borrowed a copy from the library or from another teacher. Talk about some of the feelings, such as frustration or anger, that we may have when we make mistakes, as well as the feelings, such as pride, that we may experience when we are able to solve a problem.

As a class, using Transparency 2, solve two typical study problems. Read the first problem aloud and ask students for their suggestions. What advice would they give? In the first problem, Desiree feels sleepy when she works on her homework for a long time. Students might suggest, "She should do her homework in the afternoon, so that she won't be tired." "She should work at her desk with a good light." "Don't do homework on your bed—it makes you sleepy." Record the suggestions, and then have the class write a response together. Continue to the second problem.

## ◔ Using the Reproducible

Give each student a copy of the *How Would You Solve These Problems?* Reproducible (page 27). Ask them to work together in small groups to complete the questions.

## ◔ Sharing Ideas

Ask each group to take turns sharing their answers to each problem situation. Is there more than one way to solve each problem? Does the solution sometimes depend on the circumstances? Be sure to let students know that the solution they choose is less important than learning how to face a problem and overcome it.

## ◔◔ Extending the Activity

▶ Invite students to share their own studying obstacles. Are they similar to or different from the problems described here?

▶ Have the class make a list of "Homework Bloopers and Solutions" to post in the classroom where everyone can see it as a visual reminder.

Name _____  Date _____

ACTIVITY 6

# Obstacles to Concentration—Internal and External

Think about times you've had trouble concentrating when you were studying. What distracts you? What can you do to get back on track?

| **External Obstacles:** | **What I can do to overcome them:** |
|---|---|
| 1. _____ | _____ |
| 2. _____ | _____ |
| 3. _____ | _____ |
| 4. _____ | _____ |
| 5. _____ | _____ |
| 6. _____ | _____ |
| 7. _____ | _____ |

| **Internal Obstacles:** | **What I can do to overcome them:** |
|---|---|
| 1. _____ | _____ |
| 2. _____ | _____ |
| 3. _____ | _____ |
| 4. _____ | _____ |
| 5. _____ | _____ |
| 6. _____ | _____ |
| 7. _____ | _____ |

*Overhead Teaching Kit: Study Skills*  Scholastic Teaching Resources

ACTIVITY 7

# My Study Environment Quiz

Read each of the following statements and mark them as either
True (T) or False (F). Be sure to respond honestly. This will help you
assess your own study habits.

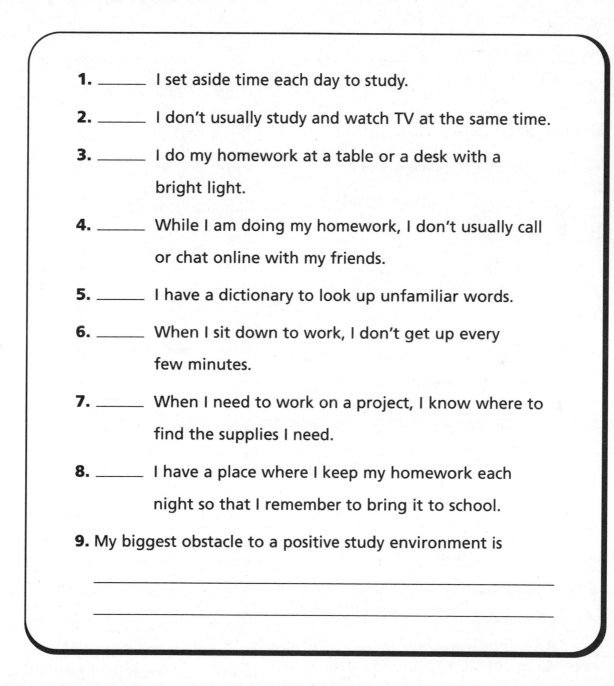

1. _____ I set aside time each day to study.

2. _____ I don't usually study and watch TV at the same time.

3. _____ I do my homework at a table or a desk with a
bright light.

4. _____ While I am doing my homework, I don't usually call
or chat online with my friends.

5. _____ I have a dictionary to look up unfamiliar words.

6. _____ When I sit down to work, I don't get up every
few minutes.

7. _____ When I need to work on a project, I know where to
find the supplies I need.

8. _____ I have a place where I keep my homework each
night so that I remember to bring it to school.

9. My biggest obstacle to a positive study environment is

_____

_____

Name _____     Date _____

**ACTIVITY 8**

# How I Study Best: My Study Plan

Answer the questions below to help you determine your own good study plan.
You may check all answers that apply.

**1.** The place I study best is

☐ my room.
☐ the kitchen table.
☐ the library.
☐ the dining room.

☐ another place: _____.

**2.** The reason I choose this place to study

is _____.

**3.** The time I study best is

☐ right after school.
☐ early in the morning.
☐ after dinner.

☐ another time: _____.

**4.** The reason this time is best for me is

_____.

**5.** I study best

☐ by myself.
☐ in a study group.
☐ with a parent.
☐ with my brother/sister.

**6.** I need a study break

☐ every 15 minutes.
☐ every 30 minutes.
☐ every 45 minutes.
☐ every hour.

**7.** When I take a break, I_____

_____.

**8.** Each day, I need to study for this
length of time in each of my subjects.

Math _____

Science _____

Social Studies _____

Language Arts _____

Other: _____

Other: _____

**9.** List 10 items you need in your study
environment in order to be an
organized and effective learner.

1. _____
2. _____
3. _____
4. _____
5. _____
6. _____
7. _____
8. _____
9. _____
10. _____

**10.** On another sheet of paper,
draw a picture of your best study
environment.

*Overhead Teaching Kit: Study Skills   Scholastic Teaching Resources*

ACTIVITY 9

# How Would You Solve These Problems?

Each of the students below is facing an organizational problem or obstacle to studying. What advice would you give each of these students?

**1.** Whenever Jennifer needs scissors or tape for her homework, or even a new pencil, she spends a lot of time looking all over her house for the supplies she needs.

✔ _____
✔ _____
✔ _____
✔ _____

**2.** Jonathan often forgets to write down what he has for homework. Then, later, he isn't sure what to do.

✔ _____
✔ _____
✔ _____
✔ _____

**3.** Last night Madison was about to do her homework when a friend called and then her favorite show was on. Three hours later, it was time for bed and Madison did not have her homework done.

✔ _____
✔ _____
✔ _____
✔ _____

Overhead Teaching Kit: Study Skills   Scholastic Teaching Resources

# CHAPTER 3

# Managing Time—
## Learning to Stay on Top of It All

Learning to manage your time well is a key skill for success at school as well as in the work world. Give students a head start by spending some of your classroom time on time management. By incorporating specific calendar and daily-planner routines into your classroom life, you are helping students establish important life skills that will serve them well in the years ahead.

This chapter is filled with activities and exercises designed to help students become more aware of how they spend their time, and learn to structure and plan their study time more effectively.

**ACTIVITY 10**   PLOTTING THE USE OF STUDY TIME

# How Do I Spend My Time?

For young children, time is elastic. A Saturday afternoon spent playing outside may pass in a blur or seem to stretch into a summer's worth of adventures. As they enter middle school, many children have not yet developed the ability to estimate the passage of time. Learning to plan time and spend it effectively are important skills that we all need to learn and use throughout our lives.

## ▶ How to Begin

Talk briefly with students about how they spend their time. Ask them to estimate how much time they spend sleeping, eating, playing sports, and so on. Have students do the math to come up with averages for the class. Record these estimates and save them for later comparisons.

Have the class conduct their own "research study" to learn whether their estimates are correct. Over several days, every member of the class will keep track of how they spend their time away from school. They may be surprised at the results.

Using Transparency 3, model for students how they might fill in their own sheets. Block out time spent in school. Then, using your own schedule or the students' estimates, block out the rest of the time using different-colored overhead transparency markers. For example, mark sleep hours in blue, television time in red, sports time in green, and so on.

## ▶ Using the Reproducible

Give each student multiple copies of the *Keeping Track of My Time* Reproducible (page 36). Ask them to record carefully how they spend each hour of each day over a period of one week. After the study is finished, have students use markers to color code their daily charts for easier interpretation, in order to create a visual presentation of time spent and to make discoveries and observations about their choices.

## ▶▶ Extending the Activity

▶ Have students keep track of how they spend their Saturday and Sunday.

**ACTIVITY 11**    PLANNING YOUR STUDY TIME

# Where Does the Time Go?

With this follow-up activity, students look closely at their time sheets and make observations about how the choices they make determine how they spend their time. When they assess how they spend their time outside of school, many children may be surprised at the discoveries they make. Use this activity to spark discussion and as a bridge for students to set new goals for their study time.

## ▶ How to Begin

Let students know that for this activity they will refer to their *Keeping Track of My Time* activity sheets. Explain that once they understand clearly how they spend their time outside of school, they can make positive changes, if necessary.

## ▶ Using the Reproducible

Give each student a copy of the *Where Has the Time Gone?* Reproducible (page 37) for homework. Have them use their time charts from the previous days as guides. Let them know that their time assessments are private and will not be shared with the class. This gives students a chance to think about how they use their time and how to make positive changes.

## ▶▶ Extending the Activity

▶ Have students write in their journals about what they learned from this exercise. You might give them a writing prompt such as, "One thing I need to change about how I use my time is . . . ."

▶ If students are comfortable sharing their time assessments, use them for math and graphing activities. How many total hours did the class spend studying for a test? Post the figure for everyone to see. What is the average number of hours that class members spend watching television? Challenge them to bring this number down.

**ACTIVITY 12**    **KEEPING ON TOP OF TASKS**

# Making a "To Do" List

List-making is an important organizational skill for both students and teachers! We use lists to remind us of the daily tasks we need to accomplish either at home or at work. Help students learn to set and prioritize goals by teaching them how to make a "To Do" list.

## ▶ How to Begin

Ask students to help make a list of everything the class needs or wants to do today. Prompt them to recall all the activities and projects the class has in progress. Include other daily events such as lunch, physical education, read-aloud time, and dismissal. List all ideas on the board or overhead. Then go over the list together. Do all the items belong on the list for today? Could some of them be held over or placed on a "To Do This Week" list? Together, using Transparency 4, make a final "To Do" list for the class to follow. Be sure to check off each item as it is completed.

## ▶ Using the Reproducible

Give each student several copies of the *Making a "To Do" List* Reproducible (page 38). Ask each student to use it to list his or her after-school activities and responsibilities. Then have students rate the importance and urgency of each activity on a scale of 1–5 with "5" being the most important. You may want to have students remove all the items rated 1 or 2 and rewrite their lists. Encourage students to make them as accurate and realistic as possible.

## ▶▶ Extending the Activity

▶ Have students estimate the time each item on their "To Do" lists will take, and then make a schedule for the evening. Do they have enough time to accomplish the items on their lists?

▶ Encourage students to estimate the time they will need to complete a homework assignment. Then, have them keep track of the time it *actually* took and record it as part of the homework. For example, students might estimate 20 minutes for a math assignment only to discover that they really needed 45 minutes. Try to do this frequently so students get a better picture of how to manage their time.

▶ Make writing "To Do" lists part of your daily classroom routine in order to help students get in the habit of recording their tasks for the evening. Ask students to check off each item as they accomplish it, and have a parent sign the sheet.

**ACTIVITY 13**   **LEARNING TO PLAN**

# Planning My Week

Keeping an assignment book or daily planner is a habit that students need to firmly establish by the time they are in middle school. When children move from the self-contained classroom to a schedule that cycles through five or more classrooms and teachers each day, they must learn to take responsibility for keeping track of their assignments. This is also an important step in the maturation process.

## ◗ How to Begin

Once students are adept at making a daily list of "To Do" tasks, have them brainstorm a list of school and personal responsibilities for a one-week period. Talk to students about the way to work with calendars. For example, they need to work backward to plan study time for tests, or to plan research time for a big project.

## ◗ Using the Reproducible

Give each student a copy of the *Quick Look at My Week* Reproducible (page 39), which consists of a weekly time chart. Have students work in pairs to record all upcoming school and personal responsibilities for the week. As a first step, have them make a list and then transfer each item to the calendar. Remind them to include study time for tests and preparation time for assignments as well as their due dates.

## ◗◗ Extending the Activity

▶ Have students assemble photocopies of the weekly chart to make their own binders for assignments and other important papers as well as the corresponding weekly plan.

> ▶ **Suggest that students use two pen colors:** red for school-related responsibilities; black for personal responsibilities.

**ACTIVITY 14**   **USING A MONTHLY CALENDAR**

# Sam's Busy Month

As students move along in their school careers, they will need to plan farther and farther in advance in order to accomplish all the tasks set before them. Challenge students to complete and follow a monthly calendar and study plan.

## ▶ How to Begin

Explain to students that the next step after learning how to keep track of daily and weekly responsibilities is to learn how to plan out a month. Using Transparency 5 and the list of activities from the *Sam's Busy Month* Reproducible (page 40), have students practice working with a calendar. Let students take turns filling in items on the transparency.

## ▶ Using the Reproducibles

Distribute copies of the *Sam's Busy Month* Reproducible and the *Calendar Page* Reproducible (page 41) to each student. If you are doing this as a whole-class activity, students can copy the information as you go to use later for an example. Otherwise, divide students into pairs to complete the calendar.

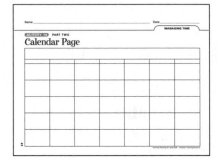

Then give each student a second copy of the blank monthly calendar and ask them to work together to brainstorm a list of their own school responsibilities and important events.

---

▶ Encourage students to use strategies to plan ahead, such as working backward from the date of a test to plan study time.

▶ Have students make a list and check off each activity as they enter it on their calendar. Remind them to include extra-help sessions.

▶ Suggest that students think and plan aloud with a partner. Articulating the process of planning their time will help them become more attuned to the assumptions and decisions they are making.

**ACTIVITY 15**   TIME MANAGEMENT TIPS AND TRICKS

# Solve These Problems

Learning to manage time is an ongoing process. Everyone experiences time conflicts. For example, on your lunch hour you might need to eat lunch, return a call to a parent, and prep for an afternoon project. It can feel as if we need to be in two places at once to get everything done.

Help students understand that succeeding at time management will require them to draw upon their critical-thinking skills and their self-discipline.

## ▷ How to Begin

Talk to students about an occasion when you found it difficult to manage your time. Discuss some of the feelings that we might have during a time crunch: stress, worry, irritation, and sometimes even exhilaration.

Next, read the following problem aloud:

> It's soccer season and Henry is having a hard time getting his homework done. When Henry gets home from practice, it is time for dinner. Afterward he watches TV for one hour and practices his trumpet for an hour. By then, it is after nine o'clock and Henry has to go to bed by ten. How can he get his homework done?

Ask students for their suggestions. What advice would they give? Use this question to spark discussion. Record and categorize their suggestions as they make them.

## ▷ Using the Reproducible

Give each student a copy of the *How Would You Solve This Problem?* Reproducible (page 42). Each problem is open-ended, and more than one solution is possible. Ask the class to work together in small groups to complete the questions.

## ▷▷ Extending the Activity

▶ Invite each group of students to write their own time management problem and share it with the class.

▶ When visitors come to your classroom, invite them to talk about how they manage their time and schedules. It is important for students to see that everyone has responsibilities and must manage their time accordingly.

Name _____    Date _____

**ACTIVITY 10**

# Keeping Track of My Time

| | |
|---|---|
| **12:00** MIDNIGHT _____ | **12:00** NOON _____ |
| **12:30** A.M. _____ | **12:30** P.M. _____ |
| **1:00** A.M. _____ | **1:00** P.M. _____ |
| **1:30** A.M. _____ | **1:30** P.M. _____ |
| **2:00** A.M. _____ | **2:00** P.M. _____ |
| **2:30** A.M. _____ | **2:30** P.M. _____ |
| **3:00** A.M. _____ | **3:00** P.M. _____ |
| **3:30** A.M. _____ | **3:30** P.M. _____ |
| **4:00** A.M. _____ | **4:00** P.M. _____ |
| **4:30** A.M. _____ | **4:30** P.M. _____ |
| **5:00** A.M. _____ | **5:00** P.M. _____ |
| **5:30** A.M. _____ | **5:30** P.M. _____ |
| **6:00** A.M. _____ | **6:00** P.M. _____ |
| **6:30** A.M. _____ | **6:30** P.M. _____ |
| **7:00** A.M. _____ | **7:00** P.M. _____ |
| **7:30** A.M. _____ | **7:30** P.M. _____ |
| **8:00** A.M. _____ | **8:00** P.M. _____ |
| **8:30** A.M. _____ | **8:30** P.M. _____ |
| **9:00** A.M. _____ | **9:00** P.M. _____ |
| **9:30** A.M. _____ | **9:30** P.M. _____ |
| **10:00** A.M. _____ | **10:00** P.M. _____ |
| **10:30** A.M. _____ | **10:30** P.M. _____ |
| **11:00** A.M. _____ | **11:00** P.M. _____ |
| **11:30** A.M. _____ | **11:30** P.M. _____ |

*Overhead Teaching Kit: Study Skills* Scholastic Teaching Resources

Name_____  Date_____

**ACTIVITY 11**

# Where Has the Time Gone?

You may be surprised after you have been filling in your time chart for several days. Take a close look at the results. Then reflect on the questions below and answer them as completely as possible.

1. On which activity did you spend the most time?

_____

_____

2. How much time did you spend watching TV? Chatting online with friends? Playing video games?

_____

_____

_____

3. How much time did you spend on your schoolwork? Reading for pleasure?

_____

_____

4. What time did you usually go to sleep? Are you sleeping at least nine hours each night?

_____

_____

5. Which activities did you plan ahead of time?

_____

_____

_____

6. Which activities were unplanned?

_____

_____

7. Which activity do you think was the best use of your time? Why?

_____

_____

8. Which activity was the worst use of your time? Why?

_____

_____

9. Is there an activity you'd like to do (or do more of) that does not appear on this list? What is it? How important is it to you?

_____

_____

10. What is the most important thing you learned about the way you use your time?

_____

_____

_____

*Overhead Teaching Kit: Study Skills   Scholastic Teaching Resources*

Name _____ Date _____

**ACTIVITY 12**

# Making a "To Do" List

## Things to Do Today!    Date _____

**I need to:**                                              **Importance 1–5**

1. _____    _____

2. _____    _____

3. _____    _____

4. _____    _____

5. _____    _____

6. _____    _____

7. _____    _____

**I want to:**                                              **Importance 1–5**

1. _____    _____

2. _____    _____

3. _____    _____

Overhead Teaching Kit: Study Skills  Scholastic Teaching Resources

# Quick Look at My Week

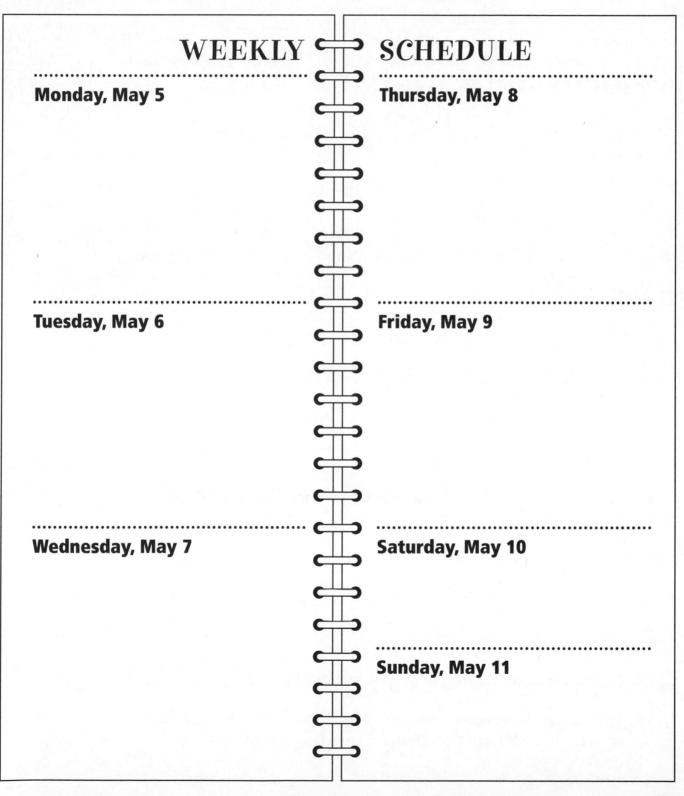

WEEKLY SCHEDULE

**Monday, May 5**

**Thursday, May 8**

**Tuesday, May 6**

**Friday, May 9**

**Wednesday, May 7**

**Saturday, May 10**

**Sunday, May 11**

Overhead Teaching Kit: Study Skills   Scholastic Teaching Resources

# Sam's Busy Month

Sam is very busy this November. On the blank calendar page provided, fill in the dates for November with the 1st beginning on a Thursday. Then fill in Sam's activities. You may abbreviate words to fit the boxes. Remember to check off each activity after you put it on Sam's calendar.

☐ **1.** Basketball practice every Tuesday and Thursday at 4:00 P.M.

☐ **2.** Math test on the 9th.

☐ **3.** Mom's birthday on the 10th.

☐ **4.** Visit grandparents for the weekend—third weekend of the month.

☐ **5.** Dinner at Jaime's house on the 13th.

☐ **6.** Science quiz on the 14th.

☐ **7.** Best friend's birthday party on the 16th at 7:30 P.M.

☐ **8.** Social studies report due on the 21st (research, type, make cover).

☐ **9.** Basketball game on the 3rd.

☐ **10.** School closed on the 6th for teacher conferences. Baby-sit for younger brother.

☐ **11.** School closed on the 12th—Veterans Day (library will be closed).

☐ **12.** Meet with math tutor every Monday at 5:00 P.M.

☐ **13.** Science project due on the 26th.

☐ **14.** Orthodontist appointment at 5:30 P.M. on the 15th.

☐ **15.** Thanksgiving vacation from the 22nd to the 25th. Thanksgiving dinner at Sam's house on Thanksgiving Day at 1:00 P.M.

*Overhead Teaching Kit: Study Skills  Scholastic Teaching Resources*

Name _____  Date _____

ACTIVITY 14   PART TWO

# Calendar Page

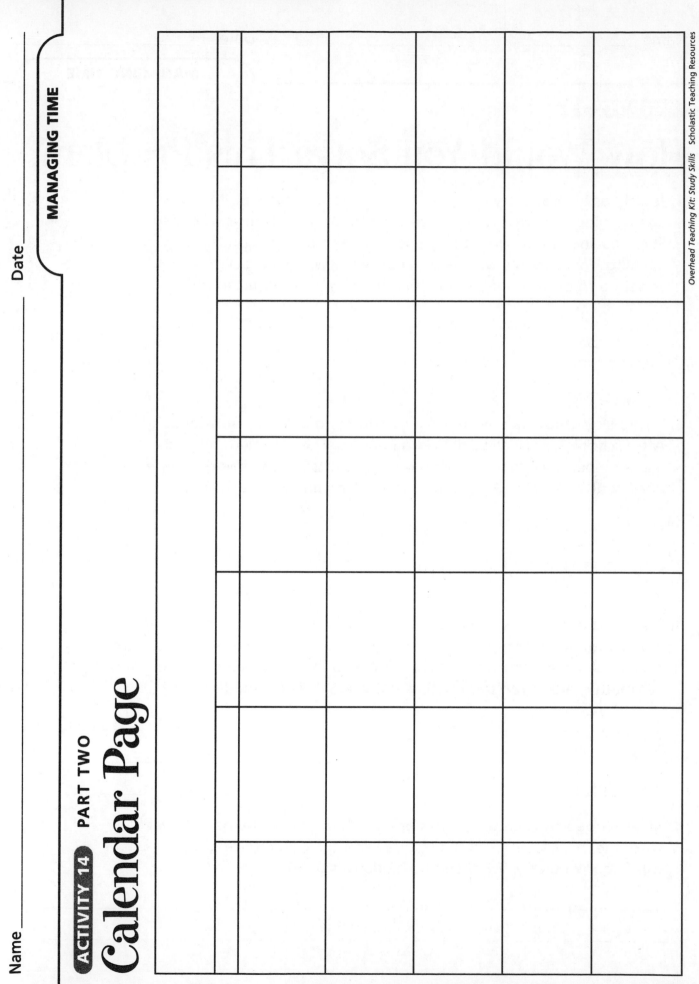

Overhead Teaching Kit: Study Skills   Scholastic Teaching Resources

**ACTIVITY 15**

# How Would You Solve This Problem?

**1.** Jewel has a vocabulary quiz and a science report due next Monday. She is going with her family to visit her grandparents next weekend. She's leaving Saturday morning and will be home late Sunday evening. Family plans will keep her busy the whole time. What should Jewel do to be sure she's ready for school on Monday morning?

_____

_____

_____

**2.** Bruno likes study hall because he gets to hang out with his friends. After school, he has a job delivering papers. Then he helps his dad make dinner and clean up. Afterward he starts his homework but he doesn't always finish. How can Bruno better manage his time?

_____

_____

_____

**3.** Sareeta spends almost every evening at her computer working on her homework. In between working on her homework, she chats online with her friends. Sareeta is frustrated because she's at her desk "all the time," and her math grades aren't as good as last year's. What should she do?

_____

_____

_____

**4.** Mike is not a fast reader. He has one week to read a 140-page novel. Last time, he waited until the last day and then tried to read the whole book quickly. What should he do this time?

_____

_____

_____

Overhead Teaching Kit: Study Skills  Scholastic Teaching Resources

# CHAPTER 4

# Reading and Note-taking—

## The Private Eye's Guide

This chapter is filled with activities and exercises designed to help students learn how to read actively. Active readers pay close attention to the features of the text. They check regularly to make sure they understand what they are reading by asking themselves questions or rephrasing the text in their own words. They take effective notes to maximize retention of the material. Like detectives, they *investigate*, they *ask questions (interrogate)*, they make sure they *apprehend* answers, and they know how to *state the evidence*. These are the reading skills that will serve students well now and in the future.

**ACTIVITY 16**   SURVEYING THE CHAPTER

# Investigating the Text

When you teach students to read like investigators you will be teaching them an invaluable skill. Help students understand that reading and learning are active—not passive—activities by specifically teaching nonfiction reading skills.

## ▶ How to Begin

Explain to students that reading to learn—reading to really understand the information contained in the text—is not the same as leisure reading. It is an active process with steps to follow. As such, they are investigators in search of answers! And like all investigators, they need a method: *Investigate, Interrogate, Apprehend, State the Evidence*. These next few lessons will teach them each step in the method.

## ▶ Using the Reproducible

The first step is investigating the text. Share the *Prereading Investigation* Reproducible (page 49) with students. Ask them to turn to a new chapter in their social studies text or to an extended passage of nonfiction from a trade book or children's magazine that relates to a current unit. Ask students to work in pairs on the prereading investigation. Remind students not to read the whole text yet, because this is the preliminary investigation! The goal here is to learn *about* the upcoming reading.

## ▶▶ Extending the Activity

▶ Go through these prereading techniques with students using several different types of text. Use the title, subheads, pictures, and other text details to encourage them to think aloud about the subject of the text before they read.

▶ Help students incorporate the use of nonfiction text features into their own writing. Once they are familiar with the steps, ask them to look at a piece of their own writing. Does the title tell the reader what it is about? Have they included helpful subheads, illustrations, labels, maps, and so on.

**ACTIVITY 17**   FINDING IMPORTANT FACTS AND CENTRAL IDEAS

# Interrogating the Text and Apprehending the Answers

Active reading involves reading with a purpose—having a sense of what you want to know and what answers you need. Too often, students approach reading with little sense of purpose. They are unsure of what they need to know and what questions to ask. Help students learn to read as if they were detectives on a case looking for clues. There are answers and they need to find them!

## ▶ How to Begin

Explain to students that in this lesson they will be learning to take charge of their own reading. It is their mission to find the answers. Reading should not just *happen* to them. They must *interrogate* and *apprehend* the text.

Start by modeling the process with students using a page or two of nonfiction text. As you read the passage together, have them work as a class to identify the main point of the first paragraph. Ask a student to record the point on the board or overhead. Then ask a second student to rephrase this main point as a question. A third student records the answer. Continue until each student has had a turn recording or until you have finished the passage.

## ▶ Using the Reproducible

Share the *Interrogating the Text and Apprehending the Answers* Reproducible (page 50) with students. Ask them to work in pairs reading a nonfiction article that relates to a current unit or a chapter from your social studies or science text. Have them work together to record the main points of each paragraph, as well as the follow-up questions and answers on their reproducible. Encourage them to include important names, dates, and/or terms in their main points, questions, and answers. When they have finished, encourage students to share their questions and answers. Ask: "How is this list useful to you? How could you use it to study? How could you use it to find a topic for writing?"

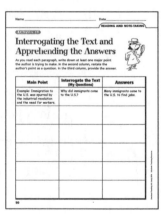

## ▶▶ Extending the Activity

▶ Have students use their completed reproducibles as notes for an open-book test or essay. Be sure to ask questions that will require them to synthesize the information and make inferences.

▶ Have students start a reading notebook using a three-column format to regularly record their questions and answers.

**ACTIVITY 18**    MAKING STUDY AIDS

# Stating the Evidence

Many students don't use their study time effectively because they don't have the right tools for studying. The best way for them to learn information is to say or write it *themselves*. Help students to learn what study methods work for them and to work those methods!

## ▶ How to Begin

Talk to students about how they study. Ask: "What helps you learn and remember new information? Does it help to read your notes aloud? Do you think about the subject while you are riding the bus or riding your bike? Does it help to have a study partner and ask questions back and forth?" List their responses together. Encourage students to think of as many possible study methods or aids as they can. Remind them that the best studying is active and/or aloud.

## ▶ Using the Reproducibles

Share the *Stating the Evidence* Reproducibles (pages 51 and 52) with students. On them, there are several sample formats for study aids. Have students take one or two pages of their notes and prepare each type of study aid. Students can use separate sheets of paper and index cards. Afterward, ask: "Which aids did you find most useful?" Remind them that different people learn in different ways. Encourage them to think about which study aids match up best with the ways they learn best.

## ▶▶ Extending the Activity

▶ Have students turn in their individual study aids for a portion of their test grade. This can be a useful incentive for students to put their best work into the studying process.

---

▶ **A Picture Is Worth a Thousand Words:** Students particularly love creating Picture Clue Notecards. Because it's hands-on, visual, multisensory, and fun, it's especially helpful for students who have any kind of language-processing difficulty. All students have to do is close their eyes and visualize their picture when they are trying to recall information—a very powerful study strategy.

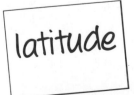

FRONT     BACK

FRONT     BACK

# Studying New Words

Have you ever noticed that even when students do well on a Friday vocabulary quiz, they often do not remember the meaning of the words on Monday? Although they studied for the quiz, they did not incorporate the new words into their own vocabularies. They did not relate the new words to one of the many thousands of words they already know. Help students *really* learn vocabulary words by helping them make connections with their own background knowledge.

## How to Begin

Start by sharing a new list of vocabulary words with students. Ask them to brainstorm ideas for learning and remembering the definitions of these new words. Ask: "How can we learn these words so that we will know them really well and can use them when we need them?" Students may mention looking them up in the dictionary, using them in a sentence, and so on.

Then, using the chart on Transparency 6, model for students how they can make an association between the new word and a *clue word* (a word they already know) that rhymes with or reminds them of the new word. For example, if the new word is *inquisitive*, the clue word might be *quiz* and a clue sentence might be "The students were curious about how they did on the quiz." Explain that some students might find it more useful to draw a picture in addition to or instead of creating a clue word. Invite a student volunteer to create a visual clue on the overhead.

Once you go through the examples one by one, as a class, come up with clues for four new vocabulary words.

## Using the Reproducible

Give each student a copy of the *Vocabulary Clues* Reproducible (page 53). Ask them to work in pairs, completing the sheet and coming up with clue words, sentences, and simple drawings. Then ask for volunteers to share their clues and their strategies with the class.

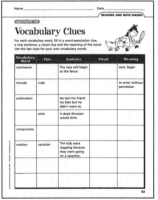

##  Extending the Activity

▶ Turn it into a game. Have a student share his or her clue word, sentence, or drawing, and challenge the class to guess the vocabulary word behind the clue.

▶ Teaching is one of the best ways to learn. Give pairs or small groups of students a list of three to five words and ask them to come up with their own way to teach their words to the rest of the class.

**ACTIVITY 20**   USING CONTEXT CLUES

# Five Ways to Find the Meaning

The most natural way to absorb new vocabulary words is through reading. You can help students understand how readers decode unfamiliar words within a passage of text by teaching them specific strategies. The clues are ready to be found by diligent detectives!

## ▶ How to Begin

Share with students a short article from a magazine or newspaper with three to five words that are likely to be unfamiliar to the majority of your class. Alternatively, use a short passage from your social studies or science textbook. Read the passage aloud or read it chorally. Then have pairs of students list the unfamiliar words. Challenge them to do their best to guess the meaning of the unfamiliar words, using clues in the reading itself. As reading detectives, it is their job to find the clues. Afterward, invite students to share their results. Ask: "What words were unfamiliar? How did you go about determining their meanings?" Encourage students to articulate their thinking processes.

## ▶ Using the Reproducible

First, display Transparency 7 on the overhead. One by one, go over each example of how to find meaning using various context clues. Following the model in Example 1, invite student volunteers to underline the clue that helped reveal the meaning of the unfamiliar word and try to answer the question about the word's meaning.

Next, share the *Five Ways to Find the Meaning* Reproducible (page 54) with students. Review the types of clues that can help them determine the meaning of an unknown word. Then ask students to write their own example sentences. In groups, have them return to the previous reading and identify the types of clues they used to determine the meaning of unfamiliar words. Ask students, for example, if they can locate any definitions by apposition or by clues in the surrounding sentences.

## ▶▶ Extending the Activity

▶ Encourage students to practice decoding unfamiliar words using context clues. With each new reading assignment, ask them to list the unfamiliar words and the clue or method they used to determine the meanings of the words. Sometimes students may need to turn to the dictionary. When they do, encourage them to return to the passage, armed with the dictionary definition.

Name _____   Date _____

**ACTIVITY 16**

# Prereading Investigation

When you read like a detective in search of answers, the first step is a preliminary investigation of the text. You need to figure out your reading goal or purpose. Before you read your chapter or passage, follow these steps.

> **Read Like a Detective**
> Investigate
> Interrogate
> Apprehend
> State the Evidence

**1.** What is the Title? _____

Based on the title, write (in your own words) what the passage is about.

_____

_____

**2.** List the Main Subject Headings. _____

_____

Now that you've checked out the subject headings, what clues do you have about the

passage? What do you think it focus will on? _____

_____

**3.** Look at all the visuals (pictures, charts, graphs, maps, etc.). List them here.

_____

_____

**4.** Are there any words in bold print? List them here. _____

_____

**5.** Are there any questions at the end of the passage? Read them carefully.

**6.** What other features do you notice about the reading? _____

_____

_____

**ACTIVITY 17**

# Interrogating the Text and Apprehending the Answers

As you read each paragraph, write down at least one major point the author is trying to make. In the second column, restate the author's point as a question. In the third column, provide the answer.

| Main Point | Interrogate the Text (My Questions) | Answers |
|---|---|---|
| Example: Immigration to the U.S. was spurred by the industrial revolution and the need for workers. | Why did immigrants come to the U.S.? | Many immigrants came to the U.S. to find jobs. |
| | | |
| | | |
| | | |
| | | |
| | | |

Overhead Teaching Kit: Study Skills  Scholastic Teaching Resources

**ACTIVITY 18**   CREATING STUDY TOOLS

# Stating the Evidence

Taking notes is an important part of the studying process, but it is not the last step. Now you need to take the notes to the next level by putting them in your own words (and pictures). Use one or two pages of your notes and practice creating your own study tools using the methods below.

Use separate sheets of paper and index cards.

## Mnemonics:

Terms I need to know: _____

_____

_____

_____

_____

_____

My mnemonic is: _____

## Picture Clue Notecard:

Picture                    _____

Word                     _____

## Main Idea Map:

## Q and A Notecard:

Q                          _____

A                          _____

Overhead Teaching Kit: Study Skills   Scholastic Teaching Resources

ACTIVITY 18  CREATING STUDY TOOLS (CONTINUED)

# Stating the Evidence

**Outline:**

**I.** _____

    **A.** _____

        **1.** _____

        **2.** _____

        **3.** _____

    **B.** _____

        **1.** _____

        **2.** _____

        **3.** _____

**2.** _____

    **A.** _____

        **1.** _____

        **2.** _____

        **3.** _____

    **B.** _____

        **1.** _____

        **2.** _____

        **3.** _____

Overhead Teaching Kit: Study Skills  Scholastic Teaching Resources

**ACTIVITY 19**

# Vocabulary Clues

For each vocabulary word, fill in a word-association clue,
a clue sentence, a visual clue and the meaning of the word.
Use the last rows for your own vocabulary words.

| Vocabulary Word | Clue | Sentence | Visual | Meaning |
|---|---|---|---|---|
| commence | | The race will begin at the fence. | | start, begin |
| intrude | rude | | | to enter without permission |
| ambivalent | | He lent his friend his bike but he didn't want to. | | |
| | stink | A dead dinosaur would stink. | | |
| compromise | | | | |
| ovation | vacation | The kids were clapping because they were going on a vacation. | | |
| | | | | |
| | | | | |

Overhead Teaching Kit: Study Skills   Scholastic Teaching Resources

**ACTIVITY 20** **USING CONTEXT CLUES**

# Five Ways to Find the Meaning

When you come across an unfamiliar word in your reading, there is a good chance that you will find clues to the meaning of the new word right there on the page. As you read the examples, underline the clue that helped reveal the meaning of the unfamiliar word. Then write your own example sentences. Here are five context clues to look for:

**1. Apposition**   With Apposition, the meaning of the unfamiliar word immediately follows it in a phrase set off by commas.

EXAMPLE: The Romans built *aqueducts*, or stone structures, to carry water.

YOUR EXAMPLE: _____

**2. Definition Signal**   Sometimes the definition of an unfamiliar word is included in the sentence. Look for phrases such as *which means, that is, which is to say,* and *or*.

EXAMPLE: This statement of rights is called the *Magna Carta*, or "Great Charter."

YOUR EXAMPLE: _____

**3. Part of Speech**   Even when you are unfamiliar with a word, you may be able to tell what part of speech (noun, adjective, verb) the unfamiliar word plays in the sentence. Sometimes this clue can help you figure out the meaning of the word.

EXAMPLE: The *ruthless* ruler forced his subjects to obey him.

YOUR EXAMPLE: _____

**4. Sentence Context**   You may be able to discover the meaning of an unfamiliar word by paying close attention to the meaning of the rest of the words in the sentence.

EXAMPLE: Because she could not write, she hired a *scribe*.

YOUR EXAMPLE: _____

**5. Paragraph Context**   When you come across an unfamiliar word, read the paragraph again. Sometimes you will discover clues to the meaning in the surrounding sentences.

EXAMPLE: The Muslims were reading the *Koran*. Those of other religions were reading their own holy books.

YOUR EXAMPLE: _____

Overhead Teaching Kit: Study Skills   Scholastic Teaching Resources

# CHAPTER 5

# Planning Projects

## How to Complete Book Reports, Science Projects, and More

As teachers know, even students with strong organizational skills sometimes find big projects daunting. Learning to plan and follow through on multifaceted assignments is an important step for all students. Through it, they develop critical-thinking skills, and the ability to work independently.

The goal of this chapter is to help students develop a system for accomplishing multifaceted assignments without feeling overwhelmed. It is filled with activities and exercises to assist students with organizing their thinking and writing on a bigger scale.

**ACTIVITY 21**   MAKING TASKS EASIER

# SLOW Down—
# Breaking It Into Steps

Like any other activity or task, creating a project or writing a report is easier if you have a plan of action and take it slowly. Share with students this simple acronym for the steps in writing a report or other project:

**S**elect a topic
**L**earn about the topic
**O**rganize the information
**W**rite!

## ▶ How to Begin

Start by explaining to your class that a big project is really just a series of smaller assignments that add up to a big achievement. To help students grasp a step-by-step process, ask them to break down a familiar classroom routine or activity into a series of simple steps. Using Transparency 8, ask students, for example, what they consider the first step in class lunchtime. Poll as many students as possible. After consensus is reached, list the first step on the transparency. Continue having students enumerate each step, listing where it falls in the "lunchtime process." After all steps have been ordered and presented, have students read them aloud to get a sense of just how many steps are contained within simple everyday tasks.

## ▶ Using the Reproducible

Give each student a copy of the *Step-by-Step Process* Reproducible (page 61). Working in groups, have students choose another task or activity (doing a handstand, mowing the lawn, etc.) and break it down into steps for their classmates. Have each student read the steps and let the class guess the larger process at work.

## ▶▶ Extending the Activity

▶ Working on a process can be easier when it is collaborative. Have students do their first big writing project in pairs.

▶ Let the final presentation guide the form. Have students turn a science research project into a short film. A social studies research report could be a big book for younger kids.

**ACTIVITY 22**    **BRINGING IT INTO FOCUS**

# Choosing the Right Topic

One of the most wonderful aspects of teaching is seeing the interest and excitement young students have for so many different subjects and topics. Yet not all topics lend themselves to a successful student project. Help students do the prethinking and careful decision-making necessary to successfully write a paper, compose a story, or plan a research project.

## ▶ How to Begin

Talk with students about the process of choosing a topic. Is it hard, easy, or perhaps a little of both? What criteria should be used? Share examples from your own teaching. How do you choose a subject for students to study? Share your criteria with students.

Display Transparency 9 on the overhead. Talk through the examples one by one. Ask students to imagine the number of steps involved in each project. As a class, rate the examples as too broad, too narrow, or just right.

## ▶ Using the Reproducible

Distribute the *Choosing the Right Topic* Reproducible (page 62) to give students a chance to practice assessing and identifying topics as too broad, too narrow, or just right. Go over the answers as a class.

Then tell students that it is their turn to choose a subject to study and share with the class.

## ▶▶ Extending the Activity

▶ List a group of topics for students and ask each student (or group of students) to rate them on various criteria: interest level, difficulty, and so on.

▶ If students are ready to choose topics, have each student present his or her topic idea to the class, explaining why he or she chose the topic and why it is just the right size.

**ACTIVITY 23**   **LEARNING TO DO RESEARCH**

# Hunting and Gathering Information

Once students have chosen their topics, let the search for information begin! While they usually enjoy the free exploration of research material, they are often unsure how to determine which information is important. Help students learn to hunt and gather information effectively.

## ▶ How to Begin

Talk with students about all the places to gather information. Work together to make a list of possible sources: reference books (atlases, encyclopedias), trade books, the Internet, magazines, newspapers, and even television. Talk with students about using one source that they may overlook: experts. Depending on their topic, students might interview one of their parents or grandparents, a family friend, a pediatrician, or a teacher.

## ▶ Using the Reproducible

After their initial exploration, share the *Recording Your Research* Reproducible (page 63). Over the course of a week or more, have students pose a new question each day and gather two or three pieces of information. Students will quickly build up a bank of questions, facts, and ideas about their topic.

## ▶▶ Extending the Activity

▶ Students can use the information they have gathered so far as the basis for a research paper. This approach will show them that diligently gathering information, little by little, is an important (and easier) way to begin a big project.

**ACTIVITY 24**

# Writing a Thesis Statement

After students have completed some research and started to link ideas together, they need to formulate a thesis statement. Learning to write a thesis that clearly represents their ideas is an important skill that even older students and adults find difficult. Here are some ways to help students focus.

## ▶ How to Begin

Explain to students that a thesis statement is a sentence that frames an essay. It often includes a series of smaller topics that can each be more fully developed in their own paragraphs (which are framed by topic sentences). The thesis statement helps the reader stay focused to better understand how the information in the paragraphs supports the main point of the essay.

## ▶ Using the Reproducible

Introduce the *Writing a Thesis Statement* Reproducible (page 64), which presents a series of questions and answers, or thesis statements. Read the first question and answer with students, exploring the ways in which each question draws out an answer. After the students understand the process, present the next two questions with the thesis sentences hidden. Then, give each student a copy of the reproducible and let them compare their sentences with the ones on the reproducible.

Allow students to discuss why and how they chose their thesis statement. Even if they have gone astray, talking through their thinking will help them choose differently in the future.

Finally, have students work in pairs to help each other formulate a question and answers that can serve as thesis statements.

## ▶▶ Extending the Activity

▶ Choose a book, a story, or a video that the class knows well and ask each student to write down the main idea or topic of that item. Have students hand in their topics and use them to write and refine a thesis together.

▶ Have student take turns reading short passages. As the passage is read, the class can write down the main idea. Are the students' ideas similar or different? Discuss the ideas together and decide upon an answer.

# COPS to the Rescue

After students put their ideas down on paper, they often think this is the end of the process. It is never too early to teach the importance of editing and proofreading. Use this mnemonic device as a proofreading checklist they can remember and follow. Students must check their:

**C**apitalization
**O**missions and Organization
**P**unctuation
**S**pelling

## ▶ How to Begin

Write out the COPS acronym on the board or overhead and talk through each item. Explain the four-step process of reviewing their work, looking for a different kind of error each time. This is much easier for students than trying to catch all errors at once.

## ▶ Using the Reproducible

Once students understand the process, pass out colored pencils as well as the *COPS to the Rescue!* Reproducible (page 65) and ask students to complete each step of the proofreading process in a different color. This will help students track the four stages of proofreading.

## ▶▶ Extending the Activity

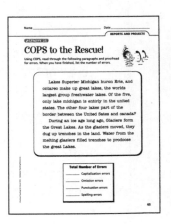

▶ After students complete the capitalization section of the proofreading process, encourage them to read the passage aloud. They may be able to pick out mistakes of omission and punctuation more easily if they hear the text.

▶ Once students are responding well to the COPS system, ask them to create their own acronyms or other mnemonic devices to help organize and remember difficult aspects of a big project.

**ACTIVITY 21**

# Step-by-Step Process

There are so many things you can do if you take it step by step! Use the map below to draw and write each step in a simple process, such as dunking a basketball, putting on your shoes, or getting ready for bed.

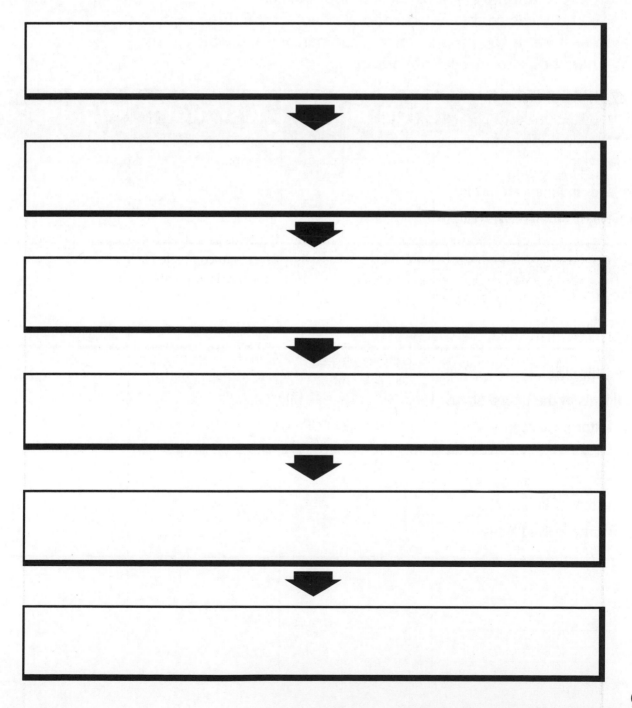

**ACTIVITY 22**

# Choosing the Right Topic

Imagining all the possible topics you could learn and write about is fun, but choosing a final topic is serious! You need a topic that is the right size for you. **Too narrow** a topic will make it difficult for you to find enough information. Choose **too broad** a topic and you will have enough information for a book or two books or ten!

Look at the choices below and decide which of the three topic ideas in each set is too broad, which is too narrow, and which is just right. Then, brainstorm a set of your own.

| TOPICS | TOO BROAD | JUST RIGHT | TOO NARROW |
|---|---|---|---|
| Boeing 747 <br> Airplanes in American History <br> The Wright Brothers' First Flight | | | |
| Life in the Oceans <br> Killer Whales <br> What Shrimp Eat | | | |
| Oval Office Desk <br> Presidents of the United States <br> Bill Clinton's Presidency | | | |
| Harry Potter <br> The History of Books <br> Harry Potter's Eyeglasses | | | |
| _____ <br> _____ | | | |

Overhead Teaching Kit: Study Skills   Scholastic Teaching Resources

Name _____ Date _____

ACTIVITY 23

# Recording Your Research

**My Topic:** _____

---

**One question I have about my topic:** _____

**This is where I looked for answers:**

| SOURCE | WHAT I LEARNED |
|---|---|
| Book: _____ | _____ |
| Magazine: _____ | _____ |
| Web Site: _____ | _____ |
| Other: _____ | _____ |

---

**One question I have about my topic:** _____

**This is where I looked for answers:**

| SOURCE | WHAT I LEARNED |
|---|---|
| Book: _____ | _____ |
| Magazine: _____ | _____ |
| Web Site: _____ | _____ |
| Other: _____ | _____ |

---

**One question I have about my topic:** _____

**This is where I looked for answers:**

| SOURCE | WHAT I LEARNED |
|---|---|
| Book: _____ | _____ |
| Magazine: _____ | _____ |
| Web Site: _____ | _____ |
| Other: _____ | _____ |

Overhead Teaching Kit: Study Skills   Scholastic Teaching Resources

Name _____ Date_____

**ACTIVITY 24**

# Writing a Thesis Statement

Q: List and describe three effects the arrival of Italian immigrants had on the culture of the United States.

A: (THESIS) The arrival of Italian immigrants affected United States' culture in many ways, including its food, architecture, and music.

Q: List and describe three ways the colonists made a living in New England.

A: (THESIS) Three ways the colonists made a living in New England were shipbuilding, fishing and whaling, and trading.

Q: Describe the main regions that make up Latin America.

A: (THESIS) The three regions that make up Latin America are Mexico and Central America, the Caribbean, and South America.

Q: Who founded the state of Rhode Island and why?

A: (THESIS) Roger Williams founded Rhode Island when he started the settlement of Providence after he was banished from Massachusetts.

.......................................................................................

**My main question:** _____

_____

_____

**My answer (Thesis):** _____

_____

_____

_____

Overhead Teaching Kit: Study Skills  Scholastic Teaching Resources

**ACTIVITY 25**

# COPS to the Rescue!

Using COPS, read through the following paragraphs and proofread for errors. When you have finished, list the number of errors.

Lakes Superier Michigan huron Erie, and ontareo make up great lakes, the worlds largest group freshwater lakes. Of the five, only lake michigan is entirly in the united states. The other four lakes part of the border between the United Sates and canada?

During an ice age long ago, Glaciers form the Great Lakes. As the glasiers moved, they dug up trenches in the land. Water from the melting glasiers filled trenches to prodoose the great Lakes.

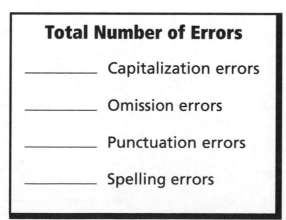

| **Total Number of Errors** |
|---|
| _____ Capitalization errors |
| _____ Omission errors |
| _____ Punctuation errors |
| _____ Spelling errors |

*Overhead Teaching Kit: Study Skills   Scholastic Teaching Resources*

# CHAPTER 6

# Taking Tests
## Different Skills for Different Tests

Taking tests—especially standardized tests—can be anxiety-provoking, even for confident students. Some children who excel in other areas of classroom participation underperform when faced with formal testing situations. There are ways you can help. Understanding how tests work—for example, knowing what kinds of questions will be asked and what strategies to use—will give students a great head start.

This chapter will help you familiarize students with different types of tests and test questions. The activities and exercises offer easy-to-remember strategies for nervous test-takers.

**ACTIVITY 26**  STEPS TO START ANY TEST

# Test-Taking Assessment

Everyone gets nervous sometimes. The more you familiarize students with types of tests and what will be expected of them on each, the less nervous and more confident they are likely to be. Take the time to build students' test-taking strategies and it will pay off in fewer mistakes, less anxiety, and more correct answers.

## ▶ How to Begin

Talk with students about how they feel about tests and what they do to prepare. Record their ideas and thoughts on the board or overhead. Explain that you are all going to work together to help every member of the class become a better test-taker.

## ▶ Using the Reproducible

Share the *Test-Taking Assessment* Reproducible (page 74 and 75) with students. Have them complete the first question, "When I take tests, I sometimes feel _____." Ask for volunteers to share their answers. List their responses and encourage them to use their imaginations to invent more serious (or silly) ways to answer the question. When everyone is ready, move on to the rest of the questions, having students work in pairs or groups.

## ▶▶ Extending the Activity

▶ Have students make posters or flyers with test-taking advice to share with the rest of the school. Sign the flyers "Courtesy of the Super Test-Takers in Room ____."

▶ Have students do a few (three to five) standardized test questions each day. Afterward have a quick discussion in which the students review and discuss which test-taking strategies they used.

▶ Have students write creative stories in which they use the adjectives and phrases generated by their feelings about the test-taking questions. Encourage them to use as many of the adjectives and phrases as they can.

**ACTIVITY 27**    KINDS OF TESTS AND TEST QUESTIONS

# The Right Skills for the Right Style

After students have explored some general approaches to test-taking, spend some time building students' familiarity with types of tests and test questions. Aim for automatic recognition—as soon as students see a test question, they will know exactly what to do.

## ▶ How to Begin

Review the main types of test questions with students. You may also wish to add more specific types: analogy, grouping ("three of these belong together"), logic questions, and so on. Have students work in teams, each concentrating on one type of question. Ask each team to create a game that teaches the strategies for answering their type of question. For example, one team will work on a true/false game, another on a short-answer game. Give them supplies to work with, such as sample tests, scrap paper, markers, and index cards. When students have completed their games, have each team present their game and teach the rest of the class how to play. Set up round-robin stations so that everyone can practice.

## ▶ Using the Reproducible

For a quick review, share the *Top Test-Taking Tips* Reproducible (page 76) with students. After you talk through the answers with your class, challenge each of your teams to come up with two questions to add to the tips quiz. You may want them to create mnemonic devices in order to memorize test-taking tips.

## ▶▶ Extending the Activity

▶ Ask students which types of questions they think are the easiest to handle and which are the most difficult. Break the class into smaller groups to discuss these types, and challenge them to explain to each other why some are easier to handle.

▶ While the students are in groups, encourage them to go through the type-specific strategies one by one and come up with additional strategies.

▶ Generate two or three questions on the board or overhead and present each one as a True/False question, a Multiple Choice, a Sentence Completion, and a Matching format. Encourage students to articulate the differences among them.

**ACTIVITY 28**    KEY WORDS

# Seeking the Heart of a Question

An important part of the work of a good test-taker is being a good reader. Learning to read each part of a test thoroughly and carefully is a skill and a habit students will need to develop. Start with the directions. Help students read directions to identify the key words that will tell them what to do. Those key words will be the foundation for the answers that they write on any test.

## ▶ How to Begin

Do a simple physical exercise with students to demonstrate the importance of paying close attention to directions: play "Simon Says" or do the Hokey Pokey. Or, challenge students to follow a scavenger hunt around your classroom. Show them that listening, reading, and remembering directions are real work.

## ▶ Using the Reproducible

Explain to students that they can use key words to learn where to go next and what to do, just as they would use a map to find their way around a new place. Share the *Key Words* Reproducible (page 77). Ask them to read each set of directions carefully and find the key words. Explain that not everyone will agree on which words are "key." They must each choose the words that help them figure out what to do. After students complete the reproducible, review it carefully with them. Encourage them to articulate why they chose the words they did.

## ▶▶ Extending the Activity

▶ Make identifying key words when you read directions part of students' daily routine. Do it with worksheets, with craft directions, and with test or essay directions.

▶ List key words that students come across every day—STOP, School Crossing, Do Not Touch! Hot and Cold—as examples of the way words are used very directly and are a constant part of our lives.

**ACTIVITY 29**

# The Writing Test

Learning to write test answers is a different skill from learning other kinds of writing, such as story and report writing. For a test, the ability to be clear, accurate, and thorough is very important. Help students improve their writing skills on tests by demonstrating and practicing writing strategies.

## ▶ How to Begin

Talk with students about the writing they do on tests. What is different about it? (For example, no time to erase or edit, have to get it right, no computer spelling check, etc.) What is good about it? (Some children might share that they find it easier to write when they have to write RIGHT NOW!)

Explain to them that one of the ways students lose the most points on written tests is by not following the directions (such as not writing in complete sentences or not addressing all parts of the question).

Display Transparency 10 on the overhead. Read each question aloud and ask students to respond in complete sentences. You may want to invite student volunteers to fill in their responses directly on the transparency. Once you finish the short and one-sentence answers, complete the essay answer as a whole class.

## ▶ Using the Reproducible

Distribute copies of *The Written Answer* Reproducible (page 78) to students. In it, they will be asked to write short, long, and essay responses to questions about the state in which they live. After students complete it, review it with them, paying particular attention to the requirements of each type of question.

## ▶▶ Extending the Activity

▶ Use journal-writing prompts as a chance to practice writing answers to a precise question. Spend time teaching students to outline their answer by jotting down a few notes.

▶ Give students practice turning questions into definitive statements. Take a few minutes each day. Call out a fun question and have students quickly write a full-sentence response that incorporates the question as a statement.

**ACTIVITY 30**  HOW MNEMONIC DEVICES CAN HELP

# Memory Tricks!

When studying for tests, having something to rely on can help students recall information. Help students learn to use acronyms, songs or tunes, rhyming, and visual clues as devices to trigger their thinking. These memory-assists will help them keep useful facts in their memories long after the test is over!

## ▷ How to Begin

Ask students to think about the kinds of devices they use to remember things they need to know. Break them up into smaller groups and give each group a notecard with a series of facts or vocabulary words related to a current unit you are studying. Ask each group to produce one acronym, rhyme, and/or visual clue to help them teach their facts to the rest of the class. Have a "reporter" in each group record the device and then share it with the class. These individual examples will get a conversation started and will add an air of fun to the memory game.

## ▷ Using the Reproducible

Pass out the *Using Mnemonic Devices* Reproducible (page 79). Go through the page, which has a number of examples, with the class. Work out each of the examples and then move on to exercises the students complete on their own. After students have mastered using sentence mnemonics, ask them to try using a song or rhyme. For example, have them learn the names and order of the first ten presidents by incorporating their names in a rhyming song.

## ▷▷ Extending the Activity

▶ As the year goes on, have students create mnemonics for different units of study. Gather them into a class book that students can use for review.

▶ Invite students to use picture-thinking. For example, ask students to write down the capitals of the southern states, then ask them to picture an image that corresponds to each of the capitals. Encourage them to choose vivid images. After they have completed the exercise, ask them to recite the capitals (without looking!) and see if they are easier to remember.

**ACTIVITY 31**    **MATH TEST STRATEGIES**

# Add It Up!

Because the other types of tests involve a specific kind of reading, the math skills activity is last. For students who feel they do not have an aptitude for math, these tests can seem the most anxiety-provoking of all. But as with all the other tests, familiarity, a sense of preparedness, and a calm approach to directions will help students get through their nervousness. Encourage students to pay as much attention to the words and directions in these tests as they did in the reading tests.

## ▷ How to Begin

First, talk about some characteristics of math: it is an abstract subject with a precise vocabulary, and it sometimes has a difficult format. Talking about fears will help start a conversation about students' various concerns and questions about taking math tests. Follow up with the math tips to help alleviate some of the concerns that will be raised in the discussion.

## ▷ Using the Reproducible

Share the *Super Math Test Tips* Reproducible (page 80) with students. Use this reproducible to help students learn and remember math test strategies. As you review their responses, work through the tips listed, having students write examples on the board or overhead.

## ▷▷ Extending the Activity

▶ If students will be required to take timed math tests, include a set of example problems and have students work through them on the clock. It is important that they go through this process in a relaxed setting before they are timed under pressure.

▶ Have students make a poster that displays math test strategies. Decorate it with mathematical symbols.

**ACTIVITY 26**

# Test-Taking Assessment

If you're like most people, tests sometimes make you nervous. Let's look for strategies that will help you get ready, feel confident, and do your best!

**1.** When I take tests, I sometimes feel _____

or _____, or even

_____.

**2.** What are five things test-takers should do before a big test?

✔ <u>Before a big test, test-takers need to get a good night's sleep.</u>

✔ _____

✔ _____

✔ _____

✔ _____

**3.** What are five things a test-taker can do if he or she is feeling nervous?

✔ <u>If a test-taker is feeling nervous, he/she could take deep breaths.</u>

✔ _____

✔ _____

✔ _____

✔ _____

Overhead Teaching Kit: Study Skills  Scholastic Teaching Resources

**ACTIVITY 26** (CONTINUED)

# Test-Taking Assessment

**4.** Below are seven types of test questions test-takers are likely to face. How should you answer each one?

**Type of test question**     **What the test-taker should do**

Multiple choice     _____

True/False     _____

Matching     _____

Sentence completion     _____

Short answer     _____

Math problem solving     _____

Essay     _____

**5.** Here are some strategies that successful test-takers use. Check the strategies you would like to try on your next test.

**I would like to**

☐ Read or listen to all directions.

☐ Skim through the entire test.

☐ Answer the easy questions first.

☐ Underline the important words.

☐ Look for clues.

☐ Use process of elimination.

☐ Always answer each question.

☐ Leave time to check my answers.

☐ If I don't know, guess!

*Overhead Teaching Kit: Study Skills   Scholastic Teaching Resources*

Name _____     Date _____

**ACTIVITY 27**

# Top Test-Taking Tips

From the phrase bank on the right, choose the
phrase that will best complete each statement.
Make sure you count the number of phrases before
you begin!

**Phrase Bank: Use these
phrases to fill in the sentences.**

    read all directions twice

    underline the key words

    check your answers

    can make a statement *false*

    change the question to a
      statement

    can make a statement *true*

    you are absolutely positive

    read all choices first

**1.** Before you take ANY test, you should always

_____.

**2.** When you read directions and test questions,

_____.

**3.** On true/false questions, watch out for words like
**every**, **never**, and **always**, because they

_____.

**4.** When you are writing an essay response, one way to start your answer is to

_____.

**5.** On true/false questions, look out for words such as **sometimes**, **often**, and **usually**
because they _____.

**6.** When answering multiple-choice questions, you should _____

_____.

**7.** Never change a test answer unless _____

_____.

**8.** When taking any test, try to leave time at the end to _____

_____.

Overhead Teaching Kit: Study Skills  Scholastic Teaching Resources

ACTIVITY 28

# Key Words

One way to improve your performance on tests is to learn how to decode the directions! When you are reading directions on a test, always underline the key words. Key words are very important—they are the action words (such as *choose*, *write*, or *draw*) that explain what you need to do.

Read each set of directions below and find the key words.

1. Look at the map and underline the names of the cities with a population of 1,000,000 people or more. Circle each capital city.

   **a.** look, circle

   **b.** underline, circle, cities

   **c.** look, underline, circle

   **d.** look, map, circle

2. Read the article and study the graph. Write a paragraph comparing two careers mentioned in the article. Proofread your work.

   **a.** read, study, write, proofread

   **b.** read, paragraph, proofread

   **c.** read, study, write

   **d.** write, paragraph, article

3. Listen to the recording of the orchestra. List every instrument you hear. Write a short description of each instrument.

   **a.** listen, recording, instrument

   **b.** listen, list, write

   **c.** listen, list, write, description

   **d.** record, list, write

4. Take the baton from the previous runner. Run 100 meters and hand off the baton to the next runner.

   **a.** take, runner, baton

   **b.** take, run, 100 meters

   **c.** baton, run, hand off

   **d.** take, run, hand off

5. When you finish your test, place it on my desk. Take out a book and read quietly at your desk. The choice of book is up to you. When you finish reading one chapter, summarize it in your journal.

   **a.** finish, take, choice, summarize

   **b.** finish, place on desk, book, read

   **c.** finish, place on desk, read, summarize

   **d.** test, read book, choice, chapter

*Overhead Teaching Kit: Study Skills*  Scholastic Teaching Resources

**ACTIVITY 29**

# The Written Answer

As you advance in school, you will need to be able to write longer and more complete responses to test questions. Some tests require answers of just a few words; others require a full-length essay. Be sure to read the directions carefully and give your answer in the way the test demands. Here are some examples of written test questions of different lengths.

## Short answer:

**1.** In what state do you live? _____

**2.** What is the capital of your state? _____

## One-sentence answer:
(Rephrase the question as a statement.)

**3.** What do you like best about your state? _____

_____

**4.** What do you like least about your state? _____

_____

## Essay answer:
(Be sure to answer every question.)

**5.** When you become an adult, where would you like to live? Will you continue to live in the state in which you presently live? If so, why? If not, why not?

_____

_____

_____

_____

_____

_____

Overhead Teaching Kit: Study Skills  Scholastic Teaching Resources

Name _____ Date _____

ACTIVITY 30

# Using Mnemonic Devices

Mnemonic devices are tools that help you remember information. A mnemonic can be a word or sentence, a rhyme, a song, or even a picture in your mind.

**Wily Words:** Create a new word using the first letter of each item on the list you need to recall. To remember the five Great Lakes, think of the word HOMES. Each letter is the first letter of one of the Great Lakes:

**H**uron **O**ntario **M**ichigan **E**rie **S**uperior = **HOMES**

**Silly Sentences:** Create a sentence using the first letter of each item on your list. To remember the planets, in order from the sun, use the first letter of each planet to create a sentence:

| My | Very | Excellent | Mother | Just | Served | Us | Nine | Pizzas |
|---|---|---|---|---|---|---|---|---|
| Mercury | Venus | Earth | Mars | Jupiter | Saturn | Uranus | Neptune | Pluto |

**Songs and Nursery Rhymes:** If you are trying to memorize a list of presidents, parts of the digestive system, or the characteristics of a cell, try singing it to a familiar tune, such as *Twinkle, Twinkle, Little Star* or *Mary Had a Little Lamb.*

**Rhymes and Word Associations:** Making up a rhyming phrase or a word association can help you remember the meaning of new vocabulary words.

Cease (Meaning: stop) Cecilia ceases at stop signs.

1. Create a mnemonic device to help you remember the Central American countries.
   (**B**elize, **G**uatemala, **E**l Salvador, **H**onduras, **N**icaragua, **C**osta Rica, **P**anama)

   _____  _____  _____  _____  _____  _____  _____

2. Create silly mnemonic sentences to help you remember the colonies.

   **New England Colonies** (**M**assachusetts, **C**onnecticut, **N**ew Hampshire, **R**hode Island)

   _____  _____  _____  _____

   **Middle Colonies** (**N**ew York, **N**ew Jersey, **P**ennsylvania, **D**elaware)

   _____  _____  _____  _____

   **Southern Colonies** (**M**aryland, **V**irginia, **N**orth Carolina, **S**outh Carolina, **G**eorgia)

   _____  _____  _____  _____  _____

Overhead Teaching Kit: Study Skills   Scholastic Teaching Resources

Name _____ Date _____

**ACTIVITY 31**

# Super Math Test Tips

From the word bank on the right, choose the phrase that best completes each statement. Make sure to count the number of phrases before you begin. Remember to check off each phrase after you have used it.

| **Answer Word Bank** |
| --- |
| multiple-choice |
| formulas |
| lowest |
| columns |
| easy |
| estimate |
| directions |
| copy |
| word |
| highest |
| skim |
| write |

1. Read all _____ carefully.

2. _____ the test quickly, writing

   down all necessary _____.

3. Make sure you _____ the

   numbers correctly on your paper.

4. Do the _____ problems first.

5. When doing _____ problems,

   draw a picture.

6. On _____ questions, solve the problems

   before looking at the answers.

7. If you are unsure, eliminate the _____ and the

   _____ answers on multiple-choice questions.

   They are usually not the correct answers.

8. If you are running out of time, _____ the answer

   and then choose the answer that is closest to that number.

9. _____ neatly and keep your

   _____ straight.

Overhead Teaching Kit: Study Skills  Scholastic Teaching Resources